RUSSIAN

Made Nice & Easy!®

Staff of Research & Education Association
Carl Fuchs, Language Program Director

Based on Language Courses developed by the
U.S. Government for Foreign Service Personnel

Research & Education Association
61 Ethel Road West
Piscataway, New Jersey 08854

RUSSIAN MADE NICE & EASY®

Year 2005 Printing

Library of Congress Control Number 00-193032

International Standard Book Number 0-87891-376-9

What This Guide Will Do For You

Whether travelling to a foreign country or to your favorite international restaurant, this *Nice & Easy* guide gives you just enough of the language to get around and be understood. Much of the material in this book was developed for government personnel who are often assigned to a foreign country on a moment's notice and need a quick introduction to the language.

In this handy and compact guide, you will find useful words and phrases, popular expressions, common greetings, and the words for numbers, money, and time. Every word or phrase is accompanied with the correct pronunciation. There is a vocabulary list for finding words quickly.

Generous margins on the pages allow you to make notes and remarks that you may find helpful.

If you expect to travel to Russia, the section on the country's history and relevant up-to-date facts will make your trip more informative and enjoyable. By keeping this guide with you, you'll be well prepared to understand as well as converse in Russian.

Carl Fuchs
Language Program Director

Contents

RUSSIA

Facts & History

Official Name: Russian Federation

Geography

Area: 17 million sq. km. (6.5 million sq. mi.); about 1.8 times the size of the U.S.

Cities: *Capital*—Moscow (pop. 9 million). *Other cities*—St. Petersburg (5 million), Novosibirsk (1.4 million), Nizhniy Novgorod (1.3 million).

Terrain: Broad plain with low hills west of Urals; vast coniferous forest and tundra in Siberia; uplands and mountains (Caucasus range) along southern borders.

Climate: Northern continental, from subarctic to subtropical.

People

Nationality: *Noun and adjective*—Russian(s).

Population (1997 est.): 147.5 million.

Annual growth rate: Negative.

Ethnic groups: Russian 81%, Tatar 4%, Ukrainian 3%, other 12%. Religion: Russian Orthodox, Islam, Judaism, Roman Catholicism, Protestant, Buddhist, other.

Language: Russian (official); more than 140 other languages and dialects. Education (total pop.): *Literacy*—98%.
Health: *Life expectancy* - 58 yrs. men, 72 yrs. women.
Work force (85 million): *Production and economic services*—84%; *government*—16%.

Government

Type: Federation.
Independence: August 24, 1991.
Constitution: December 12, 1993.
Branches: *Executive*—president, prime minister (chairman of the government). *Legislative*—Federal Assembly (Federation Council, State Duma). *Judicial*—Constitutional Court, Supreme Court, Supreme Court of Arbitration, Office of Procurator General.

Economy

GDP: $183 billion.
Growth rate: 3.2%.
Natural resources: Petroleum, natural gas, timber, furs, precious and nonferrous metals.
Agriculture: *Products*—Grain, sugarbeets, sunflower seeds, meat, dairy products.
Industry: *Types*—Complete range of manufactures: automobiles, trucks, trains, agricultural equipment, advanced aircraft, aerospace, machine and equipment products; mining and extractive industry; medical

and scientific instruments; construction equipment. *Principal U.S. imports* ($5.81 billion)—aluminum, precious stones and metals, iron, and steel.

People

Russia's area is about 17 million sq. km. (6.5 million sq. mi.). It remains the largest country in the world by more than 2.5 million sq. mi. Its population density is about 23 persons per square mile (9 per sq. km.), making it one of the most sparsely populated countries in the world. Its population is predominantly urban. Most of the roughly 150 million Russians derive from the Eastern Slavic family of peoples, whose original homeland was probably present-day Poland. Russian is the official language of Russia, and an official language in the United Nations. As the language of writers such as Tolstoy, Dostoevsky, Chekov, Pushkin, and Solzhenitsyn, it has great importance in world literature.

Moscow is the largest city (population 9 million) and is the capital of the Federation. Moscow continues to be the center of Russian government and is increasingly important as an economic and business center. Its cultural tradition is rich, and there are many museums devoted to art, literature, music, dance, history, and science. It has hundreds of churches and dozens of notable cathedrals; it has become Russia's principal magnet for foreign investment and business presence.

St. Petersburg, established in 1703 by Peter the Great as the capital of the Russian Empire, was called Petrograd during World War I, and Leningrad after 1924. In 1991, as the result of a city referendum, it was renamed St. Petersburg. Under the Tsars, the city was Russia's cultural, intellectual, commercial, financial and industrial center. After the capital was moved back to Moscow in 1918, the city's political significance declined, but it remained a cultural, scientific and military-industrial center. The Hermitage is one of the world's great fine arts museums. Finally, Vladivostok, located in the Russian Far East, is becoming an important center for trade with the Pacific Rim countries.

History of Russia

Human experience on the territory of present-day Russia dates back to Paleolithic times. Greek traders conducted extensive commerce with Scythian tribes around the shores of the Black Sea and the Crimean region. In the third century B.C., Scythians were displaced by Sarmatians, who in turn were overrun by waves of Germanic Goths. In the third century A.D., Asiatic Huns replaced the Goths and were in turn conquered by Turkic Avars in the sixth century. By the ninth century, Eastern Slavs began to settle in what is now Ukraine, Belarus and the Novgorod and Smolensk regions.

In 862, the political entity known as Kievan Rus was established in what is now Ukraine and lasted until the 12th century. In the 10th century, Christianity became the state religion under Vladimir, who adopted Greek Orthodox rites. Consequently, Byzantine culture predominated, as is evident in much of Russia's architectural, musical, and artistic heritage. Over the next centuries, various invaders assaulted the Kievan state and, finally, Mongols under Batu Khan destroyed the main population centers except for Novgorod and Pskov and prevailed over the region until 1480.

In the post-Mongol period, Muscovy gradually became the dominant principality and was able, through diplomacy and conquest, to establish suzerainty over European Russia. Ivan III (1462-1505) was able to refer to his empire as "the Third Rome" and heir to the Byzantine tradition, and a century later the Romanov dynasty was established under Tsar Mikhail in 1613.

During Peter the Great's reign (1689-1725), Russia began modernizing, and European influences spread in Russia. Peter created Western-style military forces, subordinated the Russian Orthodox Church hierarchy to the Tsar, reformed the entire governmental structure, and established the beginnings of a Western-style education system. His introduction of European customs generated nationalistic resentments in society and spawned the philosophical rivalry between "Westernizers" and nationalistic "Slavophiles" that remains a key dynamic of current Russian social and political thought. Peter's expansionist policies were continued by Catherine the Great, who established Russia as a continental power. During her reign (1762-96), power was centralized in the monarchy and administrative reforms concentrated great wealth and privilege in the hands of the Russian nobility.

Napoleon failed in his attempt in 1812 to conquer Russia after occupying Moscow; his defeat and the continental order that emerged following the Congress of Vienna (1814-15) set the stage for Russia and Austria-Hungary to dominate the affairs of eastern Europe for the next century. During the 19th century, the Russian Government sought to suppress repeated attempts at reform from within. Its economy failed to compete with those of Western countries. Russian cities were growing without an industrial base to generate employment, although emancipation of the serfs in 1861 foreshadowed urbanization and rapid industrialization late in the century. At the same time, Russia expanded across Siberia until the port of Vladivostok was opened on the Pacific coast in 1860. The Trans-Siberian Railroad opened vast frontiers to development late in the century. In the 19th century, Russian culture flourished as Russian artists made significant contributions to world literature, visual arts, dance, and music.

Imperial decline was evident in Russia's defeat in the unpopular Russo-Japanese war in 1905. Subsequent civic disturbances forced Tsar Nicholas II to grant a constitution and introduce limited democratic reforms. The government suppressed opposition and manipulated popular anger into anti-Semitic pogroms. Attempts at economic reform, such as land reform, were incomplete.

1917 Revolution and the U.S.S.R.

The ruinous effects of World War I, combined with internal pressures, sparked the March 1917 uprising, which led Tsar Nicholas II to abdicate the throne. A provisional government came to power, headed by Aleksandr Kerenskiy. On November 7, 1917, the Bolshevik Party, led by Vladimir Lenin, seized control and established the Russian Soviet Federated Socialist Republic. Civil war broke out in 1918 between Lenin's "Red" army and various "White" interventions, the Bolsheviks triumphed. After the Red army conquered Ukraine, Belorussia, Azerbaijan, Georgia, and Armenia, a new nation was formed in 1922 - the Union of Soviet Socialist Republics.

The U.S.S.R. lasted 69 years. In the 1930s, tens of millions of its citizens were collectivized under state agricultural and industrial enterprises. Millions died in political purges, the vast penal and labor system, or in state-created famines. During World War II, as many as 20 million Soviet citizens died. In 1949, the U.S.S.R. developed its own nuclear arsenal.

First among its political figures was Lenin, leader of the Bolshevik Party and head of the first Soviet Government, who died in 1924. In the late 1920s, Joseph Stalin emerged as General Secretary of the Communist Party of the Soviet Union (CPSU) amidst intraparty rivalries; he maintained complete control over Soviet domestic and international policy until his death in 1953. His successor, Nikita Khrushchev, served as Communist Party leader until he was ousted in 1964. Aleksey Kosygin became Chairman of the Council of Ministers, and Leonid Brezhnev was made First Secretary of the CPSU Central Committee in 1964, but in 1971, Brezhnev rose to become "first among equals" in a collective leadership. Brezhnev died in 1982 and was succeeded by Yuriy Andropov

(1982-84), Konstantin Chernenko (1984-85), and Mikhail Gorbachev, who resigned as Soviet President on December 25, 1991. On December 26, 1991, the U.S.S.R. was formally dissolved.

The Russian Federation

After the December 1991 dissolution of the Soviet Union, the Russian Federation became its largest successor state, inheriting its permanent seat on the United Nations Security Council, as well as the bulk of its foreign assets and debt. Boris Yeltsin was elected President of Russia by popular vote in June 1991. By the fall of 1993, politics in Russia reached a stalemate between President Yeltsin and the parliament. The parliament had succeeded in blocking, overturning, or ignoring the President's initiatives on drafting a new constitution, conducting new elections, and making further progress on democratic and economic reforms.

In a dramatic speech in September 1993, President Yeltsin dissolved the Russian parliament and called for new national elections and a new constitution. The standoff between the executive branch and opponents in the legislature turned violent in October after supporters of the parliament tried to instigate an armed insurrection. Yeltsin ordered the army to respond with force to capture the parliament building (known as the White House).

In December 1993, voters elected a new parliament and approved a new constitution that had been drafted by the Yeltsin government. Yeltsin and his hand-picked successor, Vladimir Putin, have remained the dominant political figures, although a broad array of parties — including ultra-nationalists, liberals, agrarians, and communists — have substantial representation in the parliament and compete actively in elections at all levels of government.

In late 1994, the Russian security forces launched a brutal operation in the Republic of Chechnya against rebels who were intent on separation from Russia. The protracted conflict, which received close scrutiny in the Russian media, raised serious human rights and humanitarian concerns abroad as well as within Russia. After numerous unsuccessful attempts to institute a cease-fire, in August 1996 the Russian and Chechen authorities negotiated a settlement that resulted in a complete withdrawal of Russian troops and the holding of elections in January 1997. Following an August 1999 attack into Dagestan by Chechen separatists and the September 1999 bombings of two apartment buildings in Moscow, the federal government launched a military campaign into Chechnya. By spring 2000, federal forces claimed control over Chechen territory, but fighting continues as rebel fighters regularly ambush Russian forces in the region.

Kremlin, Red Square

Wrought iron gateway

Novodevichy monastery

Hints on Pronunciation

All the words and phrases are written in a simplified spelling which you read like English. Each letter or combination of letters is used for the sound it usually stands for in English and it *always* stands for that sound. Thus, *oo* is always pronounced as it is in *too, boot, tooth, roost,* never as anything else. Say these words and then pronounce the vowel sound by itself. That is the sound you must use every time you see *oo* in the simplified spelling. If you should use some other sound—for example, the sound of *oo* in *blood* or *door*—you might be misunderstood.

Syllables that are accented, that is, pronounced louder than others, are written in capital letters.

Kremlin

Receiving hall, the Winter Palace

5

Triumph Arch on Victory Square

Curved lines (‿) are used to show sounds that are pronounced together without any break; for example, G‿DEH meaning "where."

Special Points

E *or* **EH**	as in *let*, *met*, *bell*. Be sure not to pronounce it like the *e* in *me*. Example: G‿DEH meaning "where."
I *or* **IH**	as in *hill*, *sick*, *rib*, *limb*, but you will notice that the Russian sound

is a little different from the English one. Be sure not to pronounce it like the English word "I."
Example: *chih - TIH - ree* meaning "four."

H

when underlined stands for a sound something like the one you make when you clear your throat.
Example: *beez DVOOH* meaning "minus two."

A *or* **AH**

as in *father, calm, ah, pa.* Example: *kahg-DA* meaning "when." In un-accented syllables it may sound like *a* in *sofa, China, about.* Example: *ZAHF-tra* meaning "tomorrow."

Gilded fountain, Summer Palace, St. Petersburg

The Catherine Palace at Pushkin

J stands for the sound we have in *measure, usual, division, occasion.* We have no single letter for this sound in English, so we write it in this *Phrase Book* as *j*. Remember that *j* always stands for the sound in *measure*, never for the sound in *judge*.

You will notice that consonants in Russian are frequently followed by a *y*-sound. Such combinations are like the *n‿y* sound in *canyon* or like the sounds in *view* (pronounced *V‿YOO*), *beauty* (*B‿YOO--tee*), *mule* (pronounced *M‿YOOL*), or *few* (pronounced *F‿YOO*). Consonants may be followed by a *y*-sound even at the end of a word in Russian; in this case, an apostrophe is written. Examples: *DAYN'* meaning "day," *P_YAT'* meaning "five."

You may hear slight variations in the way Russian is spoken in various regions but these differences are no greater than those you hear in different sections of our own country. It is always best to try to talk like the people among whom you happen to be.

Great Palace Church, Petrodvorets

Pavlosk Palace, Pushkin

USEFUL WORDS AND PHRASES

GREETINGS AND GENERAL PHRASES

English	*Russian*
Hello	*Z‿DRAHST-voo‿ee-tee*
Good morning	*DAW-broy OO-tra*
Good afternoon	*DAW-brih DAYN'*
Good evening	*DAW-brih VECH-eer*
Comrade	*ta-VA-reeshch*

Catherine Palace, Pushkin

The word *ta-VA-reeshch* is used with names the way we use the word "Mister" and also with titles; for example:

English	*Russian*
Comrade Pavlov	*ta-VA-reeshch PAHV-luf*
Comrade Captain	*ta-VA-reeshch ka-pee-TAHN*
How are you?	*KAHK pa-jee-VA-yee-tee?*
Fine	*ha-ra-SHAW*
Excuse me	*eez-vee-NEE-tee*

Notice that the *v*, *n* and *t* in this word are pronounced as though you were saying a *y* at the same time. Listen again and repeat: *eez-vee-NEE-tee, eez-vee-NEE-tee*. This happens in every consonant written before *e*, *ee*, or *ay* in your *Language Guide*. Try the sounds again: *vee, nee, tee*.

Please	*pa-JA-loo-sta*
Do you understand?	*pa-nee-MA-yee-tee?*
Yes	*DA*
No	*NET*

English	Russian
I understand	*pa-nee-MA-yoo*
I don't under- stand	*nee pa-nee-MA-yoo*
Speak slowly	*ga-va-REE-tee MED-leen-na*

LOCATION

When you need directions to get somewhere, you use the word for "where" along with the word for the place. For "Where is a restaurant?" you simply say "Where restaurant?"

Where	*G⏝DEH*
restaurant	*ree-sta-RAHN*
Where is a restaurant?	*G⏝DEH ree-sta-RAHN?*
hotel	*ga-STEE-neet-sa*
Where is a hotel?	*G⏝DEH ga-STEE-neet-sa?*
station	*STAHN-tsee-ya*
or if it is a large station in a big city	*vahg-ZAHL*
Where is the station?　*or*	*G⏝DEH STAHN-tsee-ya?* *G⏝DEH vahg-ZAHL?*

13

English	Russian
toilet	*oo-BAWR-na-ya*
Where is the toilet?	*G⌣DEH oo-BAWR-na-ya?*

DIRECTIONS

The answer to your question "Where is such and such?" may be "To the right" or "To the left" or "Straight ahead," so you need to know these phrases.

To the right	*na-PRA-va*
To the left	*na-LEV-a*
Straight ahead	*PR⌣YA-ma*
Please point	*pa-JA-loo-sta pa-ka-JEE-tee*

Notice the sound of *j* in the last phrase. Listen again and repeat: *pa-JA-loo-sta pa-ka-JEE-tee, pa-JA-loo-sta pa-ka-JEE-tee.* It is the same sound we have in *measure, usual, division, azure* and so on. We have no single letter for this sound in English, so we write it in your *Language Guide* as *j.* But remember! Always pronounce it as you heard it in *pa-ka-JEE-tee*, never as the *j* in judge. Try just the sound again: *j, j.*

If you are driving and ask the distance to another town it will be given to you in kilometers, not miles.

Kilometer	*kee-la-METR*

NUMBERS

You need to know the numbers.

English	*Russian*
One	*ah-DEEN*
Two	*DVA*
Three	*TREE*
Four	*chih-TIH-ree*
Five	*P⏝YAT'*

In your *Guide* the *p* is written with a *y* after it but actually the *p* and the *y* are pronounced at the same time, just as in consonants before *e, ee* and *ay*. There is also a *y*-effect in the *t* at the end of the word. Every consonant with an apostrophe after it is pronounced in this way. Listen to the word again: *P⏝YAT'*, *P⏝YAT'*. Try just the sounds again: *PEE, TEE*.

Six	*SHAYST'*
Seven	*SEM*
Eight	*VAW-seem*
Nine	*DAY-veet'*
Ten	*DAY-seet'*
Eleven	*ah-DEE-na-tsut'*

English	Russian
Twelve	*dvee-NA-tsut'*
Thirteen	*tree-NA-tsut'*
Fourteen	*chih-TIHR-na-tsut'*
Fifteen	*peet-NA-tsut'*
Sixteen	*shiss-NA-tsut'*
Seventeen	*seem-NA-tsut'*
Eighteen	*va-seem-NA-tsut'*
Nineteen	*dee-veet-NA-tsut'*
Twenty	*DVA-tsut'*

For "twenty-one," "twenty-two" and so on, you add the word for "one," "two" and so on, to the word for "twenty," just as in English.

Twenty-one	*DVA-tsut' ah-DEEN*
Twenty-two	*DVA-tsut DVA*
Thirty	*TREE-tsut'*
Forty	*SAW-ruk*
Fifty	*pay-deess-YAHT*
A hundred	*STAW*
A thousand	*TIS-ee-cha*

16

Lenin's Tomb, Red Square

WHAT'S THIS?

When you want to know the name of something you can say "What's this?" and point to the thing you mean.

English	*Russian*
What	*SHTAW*
this	*ET-a*
What's this?	*SHTAW ET-a?*

ASKING FOR THINGS

When you want something use the phrase "I want" and add the name of the thing wanted.

English	*Russian*
I want	*YA ha-CHOO*
cigarettes	*pa-pee-RAW-sih*
I want cigarettes	*YA ha-CHOO pa-pee-RAW-sih*
to eat	*KOO-shut'*
I want to eat	*YA ha-CHOO KOO-shut'*

The Winter Palace, St. Petersburg

Here are the words for some of the things you may require. They are given in exactly the form that has to be used with the phrase "I want."

English	Russian
bread	H‿LEB-a
butter	MA-sla
meat	M‿YA-sa
lamb	ba-RA-nee-nih
veal	teel-YA-tee-nih
beef	gahv-YA-dee-nih
pork	svee-NEE-nih
fish	RIB-ih
soup	SOO-poo
sour soup with meat and vege- tables	SHCHAY
hamburgers	kaht-LET-ih
eggs	ya-YEETS
milk	ma-la-KA
cheese	SIH-roo

19

English	Russian
fruit	*FROOK-tih*
vegetables	*AW-vush-chih*
potatoes	*kar-TAWSH-kee*
cabbage	*ka-POO-stih*
carrots	*mar-KAWF-kee*
cucumbers	*a-goor-TSAWF*
tomatoes	*pa-mee-DAWR*
salad	*sa-LA-too*
sugar	*SA-hur-oo*
salt	*SAW-lee*
pepper	*PAYR-tsoo*
a glass of tea	*sta-KAHN CHA-yoo*
a cup of coffee	*CHAHSH-koo KAWF-ya*
a bottle of beer	*boo-TIL-koo PEE-va*
a bottle of wine	*boo-TIL-koo vee-NA*
matches	*SPEE-chik*

Petrovsky Palace

MONEY

To find out how much things cost you say:

English	Russian
How much? *or*	*SKAWL'-ka?*
How much is it worth?	*SKAWL'-ka STAW-yeet?*

TIME

When you want to know what time it is you say really "Which hour?"

English	Russian
Which	*ka-TAW-rih*
hour	*CHAHSS*
What time is it?	*ka-TAW-rih CHAHSS?*

To say it is "one o'clock," you simply use the word for "hour."

| One o'clock | *CHAHSS* |

For "two o'clock," "three o'clock" and so forth, you say "two hours," "three hours" and so on.

| Two o'clock | *DVA chih-SA* |

For "five o'clock" and up, the word for hours is a little different.

| Five o'clock | *P⌣YAT' chih-SAWF* |

The simplest way to give the time in hours and minutes is exactly like English:

| Five twenty | *P⌣YAT' DVA-tsut'* |
| Ten thirty | *DAY-seet' TREE-tsut'* |

English	Russian
Ten fifty	*DAY-seet' pee-deess-YAT*

However, you will also hear expressions like "twenty minutes of the sixth" for "twenty after five" and "half of the sixth" for "half past five" and "minus two ten" for "two minutes to ten."

Twenty min- utes after five	*DVA-tsut' mee-NOOT shee-STAW-va*
Half past five	*pa-la-VEE-na shee-STAW-va*
Two minutes to ten	*beez dvooh̲ mee-NOOT DAY-seet'*

In the word *DVOOH̲* you heard a sound you must practice. It is written in your *Guide* as h̲ with a line under it and is like gently clearing your throat.

Listen again and repeat: *DVOOH̲, DVOOH̲*. This sound is written with simple *h* when it comes at the beginning of a syllable as in *ha-CHOO*. Try just the sound: h̲, h̲.

When you want to know when a movie starts or when a train leaves you say:

When	*kahg-DA*
the begin- ning	*na-CHA-la*
of the movie	*kar-TEE-nih*

English	Russian
When does the movie begin?	*kahg-DA na-CHA-la kar-TEE-nih?*
the train	*PAW-yeest*
it leaves	*aht-HAW-deet*
When does the train leave?	*kahg-DA aht-HAW-deet PAW-yeest?*
Yesterday	*f‿chee-RA*
Today	*see-VAWD-n‿ya*
Tomorrow	*ZAHF-tra*

The days of the week are:

Sunday	*va-skree-SAYN'-ya*
Monday	*pa-nee-DEL'-neek*
Tuesday	*F‿TAWR-neek*
Wednesday	*sree-DA*
Thursday	*cheet-VAYRK*
Friday	*P‿YAHT-neet-sa*
Saturday	*soo-BAW-ta*

24

OTHER USEFUL PHRASES

The following phrases will be useful.

English	*Russian*
How are you called? *or* What's your name?	*KAHK VAHSS za-VOOT?*
My name is___	*meen-YA za-VOOT___*
I am an American	*YA a-mee-ree-KA-neets*
How do you say *table* (or anything else) in Russian?	*KAHK ska-ZAHT' table pa-ROO-skee?*
Good-by	*da svee-DAHN-ya*

NOTE

To complete the numbers given on page 15, add the following:

Sixty	*shiz-deess-YAHT*
Seventy	*SEM-deess-yut*
Eighty	*VAW-seem-deess-yut*
Ninety	*dee-vee-NAW-sta*

ADDITIONAL EXPRESSIONS

English	Russian
English	*Russian*
Come in!	*voy-DEE-tee!*
Have a seat!	*sa-DEE-teess!*
Thank you	*spa-SEE-ba*
You're welcome	*pa-JA-loo-sta* or *nee STAW-yeet*

Note that the expressions used when someone thanks you really mean "Please" and "It isn't worth anything"—just as we say "Don't mention it" or "It's nothing."

What's your first name?	*KAHK VA-shee EEM-ya?*
What's your family name?	*KAHK VA-sha fa-MEEL-ya?*
Glad to know you	*RAHT puz-na-KAW-meet-sa*
I am your friend	*YA VAHSH DROOG*
Please repeat	*pa-JA-loo-sta puf-ta-REE-tee*
I don't know	*YA nee ZNA-yoo*
I think so	*KA-jit-sa TAHK*

English	Russian
I don't think so	*VR⌣YAHD-lee*
Maybe	*MAW-jit BIT'*
I am hungry	*YA ga-LAW-deen* *or M⌣NEH KOO-shut' HAW-chit-sa*
I am thirsty	*M⌣NEH PEET' HAW-chit-sa*
Stop!	*a-sta-na-VEE-teess!*
Come here!	*ee-DEE-tee s⌣yoo-DA!*
Right away	*see-CHAHSS*
Come quickly!	*pree-ha-DEE-tee ska-RAY!*
Go quickly!	*ee-DEE-tee ska-RAY!*
Help!	*pa-ma-GHEE-tee!*
Help me!	*pa-ma-GHEE-tee M⌣NEH!*
Bring help!	*pa-za-VEE-tee na PAW-mushch!*
I'll pay you	*YA VAHM za-pla-CHOO*
How far is the town?	*KAHK da-lee-KAW see-LAW?*

Russian dacha

English	Russian
How far is it?	*KAHK da-lee-KAW?*
Is it far?	*da-lee-KAW?*
Is it near?	*BLEES-ka lee ET-a?*
Which way is north?	*G‿DEH SEV-eer?*
Which is the road to Moscow?	*G‿DEH da-RAW-ga na mahsk-VOO?*
Draw me a map	*na-chayr-TEE-tee KAR-too*
Take me there	*pra-va-DEE-tee meen-YA too-DA*
Take me to a doctor	*pra-va-DEE-tee meen-YA G‿DAWK-ta-roo*
Take me to the hospital	*pra-va-DEE-tee meen-YA V‿GAW-spee-tul*
Danger!	*a-PA-snust'!*
Take cover!	*voo-BEJ-eesh-chee!*
Gas alarm!	*hee-MEE-chee-ska-ya tree-VAW-ga!*
Careful!	*a-sta-RAWJ-na!*
Wait a minute!	*pa-dahj-DEE-tee mee-NOO-too!*
Good luck!	*f‿see-VAW ha-RAW-shee-va!*

28

FILL-IN SENTENCES

In this section you will find a number of sentences, each containing a blank space which can be filled in with any one of the words in the list that follows. For example, in order to say "Where is the main street?" look for the phrase "Where is the___?" in the English column and find the Russian expression given beside it: *G⌣DEH___?* Then look for "main street" in the list that follows; the Russian is *GLAHV-na-ya OO-leet-sa.* Put this phrase in the blank space and you get *G⌣DEH GLAHV-na-ya OO-leet-sa?*

Notice the way in which words are put together in Russian. There are no words for "the" or "a" or "is." The word *G⌣DEH* by itself means "where," *GLAHV-na-ya OO-leet-sa* means "main street"; together they equal, "Where is the main street?" In the same way "I am an American" is *YA a-mee-ree-KA-neets,* meaning "I American."

Another thing you will notice about Russian is that the form of a word often changes according·to the way it is used in a sentence. Thus, the word for "cup" is listed as *CHAHSH-koo* because that is the form you use when you say "I want a cup" or "Give me a cup" or "Do you have a cup?" However, the simple form of "cup" is *CHAHSH-ka.* You will find the simple forms in the *Alphabetical Word List.* Still other forms of each word are used in different kinds of sentences but you needn't worry about them.

English	Russian
I want___	*YA ha-CHOO___*
I would like___	*YA ha-TEL-bih___*
We want___	*MIH ha-TEEM___*
Where can you get___?	*G‿DEH da-STAHT'___?*
Do you have___?	*ee-MAY-yee-tee lee VIH___?*
Give me___	*DA‿ee-tee M‿NEH___*
Bring me___	*pree-nee-SEE-tee M‿NEH___*
I have___	*YA ee-MAY-yoo___*
We have___	*MIH ee-MAY-yeem___*
I don't have___	*YA nee ee-MAY-yoo___*
We don't have___	*MIH nee ee-MAY-yeem___*

EXAMPLE

I want___	*YA ha-CHOO___*
water	*va-DIH*
I want water	*YA ha-CHOO va-DIH*
apples	*YA-bluk*
beans	*ba-BAWV*
boiled water	*kee-pee-CHAWN-noy va-DIH*

30

English	Russian
boiling water	*kee-peet-KOO*
butter and bread	*MA-sla ee HLEB-a*
chicken	*KOO-ree-tsih*
chocolate	*sha-ka-LA-doo*
drinking water	*va-DIH dlee peet-YA*
grapes	*vee-na-GRA-doo*
ham	*veet-chee-NIH*
onions	*LOO-koo*
pears	*GROOSH*
peas	*ga-RAW-hoo*
tea	*CHA-yoo*
watermelon	*ar-BOO-za*
a cup	*CHAHSH-koo*
a fork	*VEEL-koo*
a glass	*sta-KAHN*
a knife	*NAWJ*
a plate	*ta-REL-koo*
a spoon	*LAWSH-koo*

English	Russian
a bed	*kra-VAHT'*
a blanket	*a-dee-YA-la*
a mattress	*ma-TRAHTS*
a mosquito net	*SET-koo PRAW-teef ka-ma-RAWF*
a pillow	*pa-DOOSH-koo*
a room	*KAWM-na-too*
sheets	*PRAW-stee-nee*
a towel	*pa-la-TEN-tsa*
a cigar	*see-GA-roo*
a pipe	*TROOP-koo*
tobacco	*ta-ba-KOO*
ink	*cheer-NEE-la*
a pen	*pee-RAW*
paper	*boo-MA-gee*
a pencil	*ka-rahn-DAHSH*

English	Russian
a comb	*GRAY-been'*
hot water	*gar-YA-choy va-DIH* *or kee-peet-KOO*
a razor	*BREET-voo*
razor blades	*BREET-vee-nih-yee NAW-jik-ee*
a shaving brush	*SHCHAWT-koo dlee breet-YA*
shaving soap	*MIL-a dlee breet-YA*
soap	*MIL-a*
a toothbrush	*zoob-NOO-yoo SHCHAWT-koo*
tooth paste	*zoob-NOO-yoo PA-stoo*
a handkerchief	*na-sa-VOY pla-TAWK*
a raincoat	*duj-djee-VEEK*
a shirt	*roo-BAHSH-koo*
shoe laces	*shnoor-KEE*
shoe polish	*VAHK-soo*
shoes	*ba-TEEN-kee*
underwear	*NEEJ nee-ya beel-YAW*

English	Russian
buttons	*POO-ga-veets*
a needle	*ee-GAWL-koo*
pins	*boo-LA-vuk*
safety pins	*ahn-GLEE-skee<u>h</u> boo-LA-vuk*
thread	*NEET-kee*
adhesive tape	*PLA-steer'*
an antiseptic	*un-tee-sep-TEE-chisk-a-ya SRETST-va*
aspirin	*a-spee-REEN*
a bandage	*BEENT*
cotton	*VA-too*
a disinfectant	*dee-seen-fek-tsee-AWN-na-ya SRETST-va*
iodine	*YAW-doo*
a laxative	*sla-BEE-teel-na-va*
gasoline	*been-ZEE-noo*

I want to___	*YA ha-CHOO___*
I'd like to___	*M⌣NEH HAW-chit-sa___*
Do you want to___?	*VIH ha-TEE-tee___?*

English	Russian
I want to___	*YA ha-CHOO___*
drink	*PEET'*
I want to drink	*YA ha-CHOO PEET'*
wash	*MIT-sa*
take a bath	*VIK-oo-put-sa*
lie down	*pree-LECH*
take a rest	*a-dahh-NOOT*
sleep	*SPAHT'*
have my hair cut	*ah-STREECH-sa*
be shaved	*pa-BREET-sa*

English	Russian
Where is the ___? Where is a___?	*G‿DEH___?*

EXAMPLE

English	Russian
Where is a___?	*G‿DEH___?*
barber	*pa-reek-MA-heer*

English	Russian
Where is a barber?	G⌣DEH pa-reek-MA-heer?
dentist	zoob-NOY VRAHCH
doctor	DAWK-tur
maid	oo-BAWR-sheet-sa
mechanic	mee-HA-neek
policeman	mee-lee-tsee-ah-NAYR
porter	na-SEELSH-chik
shoemaker	sa-PAWJ-neek
tailor	part-NOY
barracks	ba-RAHK
bridge	MAWST
bus	ahf-TAW-booss
camp	LA-geer'
church	TSAYR-kuf
creek	roo-CHAY
drugstore or pharmacy	ahp-TEK-a
garage	ga-RAHJ

English	Russian
gas station	*za-PRA-vuch-noy POONKT*
grocery	*pra-dook-TAW-vih ma-ga-ZEEN*
highway	*ahf-ta-STRA-da*
hospital	*GAW-spee-tul*
house	*DAWM*
improved road	*sha-SEH*
laundry	*PRA-cheesh-na-ya*
main street	*GLAHV-na-ya OO-leet-sa*
market	*RIN-uk*
nearest settlement	*blee-JA ee-sha-ya jil-YAW*
nearest town	*blee-JA ee-shee GAW-rut*
police station	*a-dee-LAY-nee-ya mee-LEE-tsee-yee*
post office	*PAWCH-ta*
railroad	*jee LEZ-na-ya da-RAW-ga*
river	*ree-KA*
road	*da-RAW-ga*
spring	*ee-STAWCH-neek*
store	*ma-ga-ZEEN*

English	Russian
street car	*trahm-VA⌣ee*
subway	*mee-TRAW*
telegraph office	*tee-lee-GRAHF*
telephone	*tee-lee-FAWN*
town	*GAW-rut*
well	*ka-LAW-deets*

I am___	*YA___*
He is___	*AWN___*
Who is___?	*K⌣TAW___?*

EXAMPLE

I am___	*YA___*
sick	*BAW-leen*
I am sick	*YA BAW-leen*
hungry	*GAW-la-deen*
wounded *or* hurt	*RA-neen*
lost	*pa-teer-YAHL-sa*
tired	*oo-STAHL*
an American	*a-mee-ree-KA-neets*

38

English	Russian
We are___	*MIH___*
They are___	*ah-NEE___*
Are you___?	*VIH___?*

EXAMPLE

We are___	*MIH___*
sick	*bahl'-NIH*
We are sick	*MIH bahl'-NIH*
hungry	*GAW-lud-nih*
wounded *or* hurt	*RA-nee-nih*
lost	*pa-teer-YA-leess*
tired	*oo-STA-lee*
Americans	*a-mee-ree-KAHN-tsih*

That is___	*ET-a___*
Is that___?	*ET-a___?*
That is very___	*ET-a AW-chin___*
That is too___	*ET-a SLEESH-kum___*
That is not___	*ET-a nee___*

English	Russian
	EXAMPLE
That is___	*ET-a___*
expensive	*DAW-ra-ga*
That is expensive	*ET-a DAW-ra-ga*
cheap	*D⌣YAW-sha-va*
too expensive	*SLEESH-kum DAW-ra-ga*
good	*ha-ra-SHAW*
bad	*PLAW-ha*
far	*da-lee-KAW*
near	*BLEE-ska*
here	*Z⌣DAYSS'*
there	*TAHM*
clean	*CHIST-a*
dirty	*GR⌣YAZ-na*
cold	*HAW-lud-na*
hot	*ga-ree-CHAW*
warm	*teep-LAW*
large	*bal'-SHOY-a*
small	*MA-leen-ka*

IMPORTANT SIGNS

Russian	English
СТОЙ!	Stop!
МЕДЛЕННО!	Go Slow!
БЕРЕГИСЬ!	Danger!
В ОДНОМ НАПРАВЛЕНИИ!	One Way!
НЕТ ПРОЕЗДА!	No Thoroughfare!
ДЕРЖИ НАПРАВО!	Keep To The Right!
ДОРОГА РЕМОНТИРУЕТСЯ!	Road Under Construction!
ОПАСНЫЙ ПОВОРОТ!	Dangerous Curve!
БЕРЕГИСЬ ПОЕЗДА!	Look Out For Locomotive!
БЕРЕГИСЬ: ТОК ВЫСОКОГО НАПРЯЖЕНИЯ!	High Tension Lines!
ОПАСНЫЙ ПЕРЕКРЕСТОК!	Dangerous Crossing!
ПЕРЕЕЗД!	Grade Crossing!
СТОЯНКА ВОСПРЕЩАЕТСЯ!	No Parking!
ВХОД ВОСПРЕЩАЕТСЯ!	No Admittance!
ДЛЯ ЖЕНЩИН	Women
ДЛЯ МУЖЧИН	Men
КУРИТЬ ВОСПРЕЩАЕТСЯ!	No Smoking!
ПЛЕВАТЬ ВОСПРЕЩАЕТСЯ!	No Spitting!
ВХОД	Entrance
ВЫХОД	Exit
ОСТОРОЖНО!	Be Careful!

Detail, Catherine Palace, Pushkin

The Hermitage, St. Petersburg

ALPHABETICAL WORD LIST

In Russian the form of a word often changes according to the way it is used in a sentence. For example, the simple form of the word for "room"—*KAWM-na-ta*—is always used in a sentence like "This is the room," *ET-a KAWM-na-ta*. However, in a sentence like "I want a room," the word is changed to *KAWM-na-too* and you say *YA ha-CHOO KAWM-na-too*. The simple form is given in the list below. For the correct form to use in sentences like *I want ___, Give me ___*, etc. see p. 18 and 30.

English	*Russian*
	A
adhesive tape	*PLA-steer'*
after	
twenty after five	*DVA-tsut' mee-NOOT shee-STAW-va*
afternoon	
Good afternoon	*DAW-brih DAYN'*
am	
I am___	*YA___*
American	

English	Russian
American soldiers	*a-mee-ree-KAHN-skee-yee sahl-DA-tih*
I am an American	*YA a-mee-ree-KA-neets*
We are Americans	*MIH a-mee-ree-KAHN-tsih*
and	*ee*
antiseptic	*un-tee-sep-TEE-chisk-a-ya SRETST-va*
apples	*YA-bla-ka*
are	
Are you___?	*VIH___?*
They are___	*ah-NEE___*
We are___	*MIH___*
aspirin	*a-spee-REEN*

B

bad	*PLAW-ha*
bandage	*BEENT*
barber	*pa-reek-MA-heer*
barracks	*ba-RAHK*
beans	*ba-BIH*

English	Russian
bed	*kra-VAHT'*
beef	*gahv-YA-dee-na*
beer	*PEE-va*
a bottle of beer	*boo-TIL-ka PEE-va*
beginning	*nu-CHA-la*
blades	
razor blades	*BREET-vee-nih-yee NAW-jik-ee*
blanket	*a-dee-YA-la*
bottle	*boo-TIL-ka*
a bottle of beer	*boo-TIL-ka PEE-va*
boiled water	*kee-pee-CHAWN-na-ya va-DA*
bread	*H⌣LEB*
bridge	*MAWST*
bring	
Bring me___	*pree-nee-SEE-tee M⌣NEH___*
Bring help!	*pa-za-VEE-tee na PAW-mushch!*
brush	*SHCHAWT-ka*
shaving brush	*SHCHAWT-ka dlee breet-YA*

English	Russian
bus	*ahf-TAW-booss*
butter	*MA-sla*
buttons	*POO-ga-veet-sih*

C

cabbage	*ka-POO-sta*
camp	*LA-geer'*
can	
Where can you get___?	*G⌣DEH da-STAHT'___?*
captain	*ka-pee-TAHN*
Careful!	*a-sta-RAWJ-na!*
carrots	*mar-KAWF-ka*
cheap	*D⌣YAW-sha-va*
cheese	*SIHR*
chicken	*KOO-ree-Tsa*
chocolate	*sha-ka-LAHD*
church	*TSAYR-kuf*
cigarettes	*pa-pee-RAW-sih*
cigar	*see-GA-ra*
city	*GAW-rut*

English	Russian
clean	*CHIST-a*
coffee	*KAW-fee*
a cup of coffee	*CHAHSH-ka KAWF-ya*
cold	*HAW-lud-na*
comb	*GRAY-been'*
Come!	*pree-ha-DEE-tee!*
Come here!	*ee-DEE-tee s⌣yoo-DA!*
Come in!	*voy-DEE-tee!*
Come quickly!	*pree-ha-DEE-tee ska-RAY!*
comrade	*ta-VA-reeshch*
Comrade Pavlov	*ta-VA-reeshch PAHV-luf*
Comrade Captain	*ta-VA-reeshch ka-pee-TAHN*
cotton	*VA-ta*
cover	
Take cover!	*voo-BEJ-eesh-chee!*
creek	*roo-CHAY*
cucumber	*a-goo-RETS*
cup	*CHAHSH-ka*

Varvarka station

Grand Ballroom, the Winter Palace, St. Petersburg

English	Russian

D

English	Russian
Danger!	*a-PA-snust'!*
dentist	*zoob-NOY VRAHCH*
dirty	*GR‿YAZ-na*
disinfectant	*dee-seen-fek-tsee-AWN-na-ya SRETST-va*
Do you understand?	*pa-nee-MA‿ee-tee?*
doctor	*DAWK-tur*
Take me to a doctor	*pra-va-DEE-tee meen-YA G‿DAWK-ta-roo*
Draw me a map	*na-chayr-TEE-tee KAR-too*
drink	*PEET'*
drugstore	*ahp-TEK-a*

E

English	Russian
eat	*KOO-shut'*
eggs	*YA‿ee-tsa*
eight	*VAW-seem*
eighteen	*va-seem-NA-tsut'*
eighty	*VAW-seem-deess-yut*

English	Russian
eleven	*ah-DEE-na-tsut'*
evening	*VECH-eer*
Good evening	*DAW-brih VECH-eer*
Excuse me	*eez-vee-NEE-tee*
expensive	*DAW-ra-ga*
too expensive	*SLEESH-kum DAW-ra-ga*

F

family name	*fa-MEEL-ya*
What's your family name?	*KAHK VA-sha fa-MEEI -ya?*
far	*da-lee-KAW*
How far is it?	*KAHK da-lee-KAW?*
Is it far?	*da-lee-KAW?*
fifteen	*peet-NA-tsut'*
fifty	*pay-deess-YAHT*
fine	*ha-ra-SHAW*
first name	*EEM-ya*
What's your first name?	*KAHK VA-shee EEM-ya?*

English	Russian
five	*P⌣YAT'*
fish	*RIB-a*
fork	*VEEL-ka*
forty	*SAW-ruk*
four	*chih-TIH-ree*
fourteen	*chih-TIHR-na-tsut'*
Friday	*P⌣YAHT-neet-sa*
friend	*DROOG*
I am your friend	*YA VAHSH DROOG*
fruit	*FROOK-tik*

G

garage	*ga-RAHJ*
Gas alarm!	*kee-MEE-chee-ska-ya tree-VAW-ga!*
gas station	*za-PRA-vach-noy POONKT*
gasoline	*been-ZEEN*
get	
Where can you get___?	*G⌣DEH da-STAHT'___?*
Give me___	*DA⌣ee-tee M⌣NEH___*

English	Russian
Glad to know you	*RAHT puz-na-KAW-meet-sa*
glass	*sta-KAHN*
a glass of tea	*sta-KAHN CHA-yoo*
Go! *or* Move!	*ee-DEE-tee!*
Go quickly!	*ee-DEE-tee ska-RAY!*
good	*ha-RAW-shih* *or* *DAW-brih*
Good afternoon	*DAW-brih DAYN'*
Good evening	*DAW-brih VECH-eer*
Good morning	*DAW-broy OO-tra*
Good-by	*da svee-DAHN-ya*
grapes	*vee-na-GRAHD*
grocery store	*pra-dook-TAW-vih ma-ga-ZEEN*

H

hair	
have my hair cut	*ah-STREECH-sa*

English	Russian
half	*pa-la-VEE-na*
half past five	*pa-la-VEE-na shee-STAW-va*
ham	*vee-chee-NA*
hamburgers	*kaht-LET-ih*
handkerchief	*na-sa-VOY pla-TAWK*
have	
Have a seat!	*sa-DEE-teess!*
I have___	*YA ee-MAY-yoo___*
I don't have___	*YA nee ee-MAY-yoo___*
Do you have___?	*ee-MAY-yee-tee lee VIH___?*
We don't have___	*MIH nee ee-MAY-yeem___*
He	*AWN*
He is___	*AWN___*
hello	*Z‿DRAHST-voo‿ee-tee*
Help!	*pa-ma-GHEE-tee!*
Bring help!	*pa-za-VEE-tee na PAW-mushch!*
Help me!	*pa-ma-GHEE-tee M‿NEH!*

English	Russian
here	Z‿DAYSS'
This is here	E-ta Z‿DAYSS'
Come here!	ee-DEE-tee s‿yoo-DA!
highway	ahf-ta-STRA-da
hospital	GAW-spee-tul
Take me to the hospital	pra-va-DEE-tee meen-YA V‿GAW-spee-tul
hot	ga-ree-CHAW
hot water	gar-YA-cha-ya va-DA *or* kee-pee-TAWK
hotel	ga-STEE-neet-sa
Where is a hotel?	G‿DEH ga-STEE-neet-sa?
hour	CHAHSS
Which hour? *or* What time is it?	ka-TAW-rih CHAHSS?
house	DAWM
how	KAHK
How are you?	KAHK pa-jee-VA-yee-tee?
How do you say___?	KAHK ska-ZAHT'___?

54

English	Russian
How far is it?	*KAHK da-lee-KAW?*
How much?	*SKAWL'-ka?*
How much is it worth?	*SKAWL'-ka STAW-yeet?*
hundred	*STAW*
hungry	
I am hungry	*YA ga-LAW-deen* *or M⌣NEH KOO-shut' HAW-chit-sa*
hurt	*RA-neen*
I am hurt	*YA RA-neen*
We are hurt	*MIH RA-nee-nih*

I

I	*YA*
I am___	*YA___*
I am an American	*YA a-mee-ree-KA-neets*
I have___	*YA ee-MAY-yoo___*
I don't have___	*YA nee ee-MAY-yoo___*
I'd like to___	*M⌣NEH HAW-chit-sa___*

English	Russian
I want___ *or* I want to___	*YA ha-CHOO___*
I would like___	*YA ha-TEL-bih___*
improved road	*sha-SEH*
ink	*cheer-NEE-la*
in Russian	*pa-ROO-skee*
iodine	*YAWD*
is	
He is___	*AWN___*
Is it far?	*da-lee-KAW?*
That is___	*ET-a___*
That is not___	*ET-a nee___*
What's this?	*SHTAW ET-a?*

K

kilometer	*kee-la-METR*
knife	*NAWJ*
know	
I don't know	*YA nee ZNA-yoo*
kopek	*ka-PAY-ka*

Royal bed at the Pavlovsk Palace

Svato Danilov monastery

English	Russian

L

English	Russian
lamb	*ba-RA-nee-na*
large	*bal'-SHOY-a*
laundry	*PRA-cheesh-na-ya*
laxative	*sla-BEE-teel-na-ya*
leave	
When does the train leave?	*kahg-DA aht-HAW-deet PAW-yeest?*
left	
To the left	*na-LEV-a*
lie down	*pree-LECH*
like	
I'd like to___	*M⌣NEH HAW-chit-sa___*
I would like___	*YA ha-TEL bih___*
lost	
I am lost	*YA pa-teer-YAHL-sa*
We are lost	*MIH pa-teer-YA-leess*
luck	
Good luck!	*f⌣see-VAW ha-RAW-shee-val*

English	Russian

M

maid	*oo-BAWR-sheet-sa*
main street	*GLAHV-na-ya OO-leet-sa*
map	*KAR-ta*
Draw me a map	*na-chayr-TEE-tee KAR-too*
market	*RIN-uk*
matches	*SPEECH-kee*
mattress	*ma-TRAHTS*
maybe	*MAW-jit BIT'*
meat	*M⌣YA-sa*
mechanic	*mee-HA-neek*
milk	*ma-la-KAW*
minute	*mee-NOO-ta*
Wait a minute!	*pa-dahj-DEE-tee mee-NOO-too!*
Monday	*pa-nee-DEL'-neek*
morning	*OO-tra*
Good morning	*DAW-broy OO-tra*

English	Russian
mosquito net	*SET-ka PRAW-teef ka-ma-RAWF*
movie *or* picture	*kar-TEE-na*
When does the movie begin?	*kahg-DA na-CHA-la kar-TEE-nih?*

N

name	
My name is___	*meen-YA za-VOOT___*
What is your name?	*KAHK VAHSS za-VOOT?*
What's your family name?	*KAHK VA-sha fa-MEEL-ya?*
What's your first name?	*KAHK VA-shee EEM-ya?*
near	*BLEE-ska*
nearest settlement	*blee-JA ee-sha-ya jil-YAW* *or* *blee-JA ee-shee pahss-YAW-luk*
nearest town	*blee-JA ee-shee GAW-rut*
needle	*ee-GAWL-ka*
nine	*DAY-veet'*

English	Russian
nineteen	*dee-veet-NA-tsut'*
ninety	*dee-vee-NAW-sta*
no	*NET*
north	*SEV-eer*
Which way is north?	*G‿DEH SEV-eer?*
not	*nee*
I don't understand	*nee pa-nee-MA-yoo*
That is not___	*ET-a nee___*

O

o'clock	
one o'clock	*CHAHSS*
two o'clock	*DVA chih-SA*
five o'clock	*P‿YAT' chih-SAWF*
one	*ah-DEEN*
onions	*LOOK*

60

English	Russian
	P
paper	*boo-MA-ga*
pay	
I'll pay you	*YA VAHM za-pla-CHOO*
pear	*GROO-sha*
peas	*ga-RAW'H*
pen	*pee-RAW*
pencil	*ka-rahn-DAHSH*
pepper	*PAY-reets*
pillow	*pa-DOOSH-ka*
pins	*boo-LAHF-kee*
safety pins	*ahn-GLEE-skee boo-LAHF-kee*
pharmacy	*ahp-TEK-a*
pipe	*TROOP-ka*
plate	*ta-REL-ka*
please	*pa-JA-loo-sta*
Point!	*pa-ka-JEE-tee!*
policeman	*mee-lee-tsee-ah-NAYR*
police station	*a-dee-LAY-nee-ya mee-LEE-tsee-yee*
pork	*svee-NEE-na*

English	Russian
porter	*na-SEELSH-chik*
post office	*PAWCH-ta*
potatoes	*kar-TAWSH-ka*

Q

quickly

    Come quickly!   *pree-ha-DEE-tee ska-RAY!*

    Go quickly!   *ee-DEE-tee ska-RAY!*

R

railroad	*jee-LEZ-na-ya da-RAW-ga*
railroad station	*STAHN-tsee-ya*
	or *vahg-ZAHL*
raincoat	*duj-djee-VEEK*
razor	*BREET-va*
razor blades	*BREET-vee-nih-yee NAW-jik-ee*
Repeat!	*puf-ta-REE-tee!*
rest	*a-dahh-NOOT'*
restaurant	*ree-sta-RAHN*

English	Russian
Where is a restaurant?	G‿DEH ree-sta-RAHN?
right	
to the right	na-PRA-va
river	ree-KA
road	da-RAW-ga
Which is the road to Moscow?	G‿DEH da-RAW-ga na mahsk-VOO?
room	KAWM-na-ta
ruble	ROOBL'
Russian	ROO-skee
in Russian	pa-ROO-skee

S

safety pins	ahn-GLEE-skee boo-LAHF-kee
salad	sa-LAHT
salt	SAWL'
Saturday	soo-BAW-ta
seat	
Have a seat!	sa-DEE-teess!

English	Russian
settlement	*jil-YAW* or *pahss-YAW-luk*
the nearest settlement	*blee-JA⌣ee-sha-ya jil-YAW* or *blee-JA⌣ee-shee pahss-YAW-luk*
seven	*SEM*
seventeen	*seem-NA-tsut'*
seventy	*SEM-deess-yut*
shave	
be shaved	*pa-BREET-sa*
shaving brush	*SHCHAWT-ka dlee breet-YA*
shaving soap	*MIL-a dlee breet-YA*
she	*ah-NA*
sheets	*PRAW-stee-nee*
shirt	*roo-BAHSH-ka*
shoes	*ba-TEEN-kee*
shoe laces	*shnoor-KEE*
shoemaker	*sa-PAWJ-neek*
shoe polish	*VAHK-sa*

The Great Palace, Petrodvorets

Monastery at the Kremlin

English	Russian
sick	
I am sick	*YA BAW-leen*
We are sick	*MIH bahl'-NIH*
six	*SHAYST'*
sixteen	*shiss-NA-tsut'*
sixty	*shiz-deess-YAHT*
sleep	*SPAHT'*
slowly	*MED-leen-na*
Speak slowly!	*ga-va-REE-tee MED-leen-na!*
small	*MA-leen-ka*
soap	*MIL-a*
shaving soap	*MIL-a dlee breet-YA*
soldier	*sahl-DAHT*
soup	*SOOP*

Martino Park

65

English	Russian
sour soup with meat and vegetables	*SHCHEE*
Speak!	*ga-va-REE-tee!*
Speak slowly!	*ga-va-REE-tee MED-leen-na!*
spoon	*LAWSH-ka*
spring	*ee-STAWCH-neek*
start	
When does the movie start?	*kahg-DA na-CHA-la kar-TEE-nih?*
station	*STAHN-tsee-ya*
	or vahg-ZAHL
Where is the station?	*G‿DEH STAHN-tsee-ya?*
	or G‿DEH vahg-ZAHL?
police station	*a-dee-LAY-nee-ya mee-LEE-tsee-yee*
railroad station	*STAHN-tsee-ya*
	or vahg-ZAHL
Stop!	*a-sta-na-VEE-teess!*
store	*ma-ga-ZEEN*
straight ahead	*PR‿YA-ma*

English	Russian
street	*OO-leet-sa*
main street	*GLAHV-na-ya OO-leet-sa*
street-car	*trahm-VA‿ee*
subway	*mee-TRAW*
sugar	*SA-hur*
Sunday	*va-skree-SAYN-ya*

T

tailor	*part-NOY*
take	
Take cover!	*voo-BEJ-eesh-chee!*
Take me there	*pra-va-DEE-tee meen-YA too-DA*
Take me to a doctor	*pra-va-DEE-tee meen-YA G‿DAWK-ta-roo*
Take me to the hospital	*pra-va-DEE-tee meen-YA V‿GAW-spee-tul*
tea	*CHA‿ee*
a glass of tea	*sta-KAHN CHA-yoo*
telegraph office	*tee-lee-GRAHF*

67

English	Russian
telephone	*tee-lee-FAWN*
ten	*DAY-seet'*
Thank you	*spa-SEE-ba*
that or this	*ET-a*
That is___	*ET-a___*
Is that___?	*ET-a___?*
What is this?	*SHTAW ET-a?*
there	*TAHM*
they	*ah-NEE*
They are___	*ah-NEE___*
think	
I think so	*KA-jit-sa TAHK*
I don't think so	*VR⌣YAHD-lee*
thirsty	
I am thirsty	*M⌣NEH PEET' HAW-chit-sa*
thirteen	*tree-NA-tsut'*
thirty	*TREE-tsut'*
thousand	*TIS-ee-cha*
thread	*NEET-ka*

68

Duzol animal theatre

The Summer Palace, St. Petersburg

English	Russian
three	*TREE*
Thursday	*chit-VAYRK*
time	
What time is it?	*ka-TAW-rih CHAHSS?*
tired	
I am tired	*YA oo-STAHL*
We are tired	*MIH oo-STA-lee*
to	
to a doctor	*G‿DAWK-ta-roo*
to the hospital	*V‿GAW-spee-tul*
to the left	*na-LEV-a*
to the right	*na-PRA-va*
two minutes to ten	*beez DVOOH mee-NOOT DAY-seet'*
too	*SLEESH-kum*
That is too___	*ET-a SLEESH-kum___*
tobacco	*ta-BAHK*
today	*see-VAWD-n‿ya*
toilet	*oo-BAWR-na-ya*

English	Russian
English	*Russian*
Where is the toilet?	G⌣DEH oo-BAWR-na-ya?
tomato	pa-mee-DAWR
tomorrow	ZAHF-tra
too expensive	SLEESH-kum DAW-ra-ga
toothbrush	zoob-NA-ya SHCHAWT-ka
tooth paste	zoob-NA-ya PA-sta
towel	pa-la-TEN-tsa
town	GAW-rut
	or see-LAW
nearest town	blee-JA⌣ee-shee GAW-rut
train	PAW-yeest
When does the train leave?	kahg-DA aht-HAW-deet PAW-yeest?
Tuesday	F⌣TAWR-neek
twelve	dvee-NA-tsut'
twenty	DVA-tsut'
twenty-one	DVA-tsut' ah-DEEN
twenty-two	DVA-tsut DVA
two	DVA

70

English	Russian

U

understand

Do you
understand? · *pa-nee-MA-yee-tee?*

I understand · *pa-nee-MA-yoo*

I don't
understand · *nee pa-nee-MA-yoo*

underwear · *NEEJ-nee-ya beel-YAW*

V

veal · *teel-YA-tee-na*

vegetables · *AW-vush-chih*

very · *AW-chin*

That is
very___ · *ET-a AW-chin___*

W

Wait! · *pa-dahj-DEE-tee!*

Wait a
minute! · *pa-dahj-DEE-tee mee-NOO-too!*

want

English	Russian
I want___ _or_ I want to___	_YA ha-CHOO___
warm	_teep-LAW_
wash	_MIT-sa_
water	_va-DA_
boiled water	_kee-pee-CHAWN-na-ya va-DA_
boiling water	_kee-pee-TAWK_
drinking water	_va-DA dlee peet-YA_
hot water	_gar-YA-cha-ya va-DA_
watermelon	_ar-BOOZ_
we	_MIH_
We are___	_MIH___
We have___	_MIH ee-MAY-yeem___
We don't have___	_MIH nee ee-MAY-yeem____
We want___	_MIH ha-TEEM___
Wednesday	_sree-DA_
welcome	
you're welcome	_pa-JA-loo-sta_ _or_ _nee STAW-yeet_

English	Russian
well (in good health)	*ha-ra-SHAW*
well (for water)	*ka-LAW-deets*
what	*SHTAW*
What is this?	*SHTAW ET-a?*
What time is it?	*ka-TAW-rih CHAHSS?*
when	*kahg-DA*
When does the movie begin?	*kahg-DA na-CHA-la kar-TEE-nih?*
When does the train leave?	*kahg-DA aht-HAW-deet PAW-yeest?*
where	*G⌣DEH*
Where is the___?	*G⌣DEH___?*
or Where is a___?	
which	*ka-TAW-rih*
which hour	*ka-TAW-rih CHAHSS*
Which is the road to Moscow?	*G⌣DEH da-RAW-ga na mahsk-VOO?*

English	Russian
Which way is north?	*G‿DEH SEV-eer?*
who	
Who is___?	*K‿TAW___?*
wine	*vee-NAW*
a bottle of wine	*boo-TIL-ka vee-NA*
wounded	
I am wounded	*YA RA-neen*
We are wounded	*MIH RA-nee-nih*

Y

yes	*DA*
yesterday	*f‿chee-RA*

Red Square